Original title:
Meadow Murmurs

Copyright © 2025 Creative Arts Management OÜ
All rights reserved.

Author: Cassandra Whitaker
ISBN HARDBACK: 978-1-80566-677-6
ISBN PAPERBACK: 978-1-80566-962-3

Sounds of Serenity in Bloom

In fields where daisies play a game,
The butterflies dance, never the same.
Grass tickles toes in a playful jest,
A ladybug joins, looking quite impressed.

Bees buzz around like they're in a race,
Chasing the flowers, each a sweet face.
A rabbit hops past with a wink and a nod,
While a squirrel jokes with a small round clod.

The wind whispers secrets with a giggle and spin,
As daisies sway softly, letting fun begin.
A frog in a patch tries to croak a tune,
Only to be drowned by a raucous raccoon.

With laughter in petals and joy in the air,
A cloud does a flip, showing off its flair.
So come join the chorus, it's never too late,
In this funny symphony, love's always great!

Laughter in the Blooming Bay

Bumblebees buzz with a goofy flair,
While daisies gossip without a care.
A butterfly trips on its polka-dot dress,
And giggles of petals cause quite the mess.

Squirrels chase shadows, setting the pace,
As wind whips around in a playful race.
A frog in a hat croaks comedy notes,
While rabbits debate in their silly coats.

Echoes of the Earthbound

A worm in a top hat claims he's profound,
While ants in a line make a raucous sound.
The grasshoppers croon in a jocose way,
And roll on the ground, refusing to stay.

Leaves shimmy and shake, in a dance of delight,
While the daisies laugh under stars so bright.
An owl who can't hoot stumbles on words,
Tickling the funny bones of nearby birds.

A Dance of Flitting Shadows

Fireflies twinkle in a quirky parade,
With beetles on drums, they start a charade.
A shadow slips by with an exaggerated sway,
While crickets hold court on a grand cabaret.

Grass bends low, trying not to laugh,
As a snail takes a bow, embracing its path.
A jaunty raccoon draws a crowd with flair,
Singing songs of the world without a care.

Bellows of the Basalt Ridge

Atop the ridge, the wind tells a joke,
As stones take a pause, and the boulders poke.
Laughter erupts from a nearby creek,
Where tadpoles are splashing in havoc so chic.

The echoes do giggle, flitting through trees,
As a dandelion dances, tickling the bees.
A mountain goat trips and rolls down the glade,
While the flowers all chuckle at the grand escapade.

The Language of Leaves

Whispers of green, a gossiping spree,
Leaves chitchat softly as breezes run free.
They poke fun at the clouds, so poofy and fat,
While squirrels roll their eyes, in a tittersome spat.

Dancing in sunbeams, they share all their jokes,
The tall grass giggles, while mischief awokes.
Branches nod knowingly, like they're in a play,
As acorns drop down, and the birds join the fray.

Soft Sounds of the Pasture

Bovine choirs moo, in a symphonic frolic,
Chasing the crickets with rhythm so colic.
Sheep tell each other, the silliest tales,
While the wind joins the hymn, with gusts that prevail.

The daisies are laughing, such cheerful sights,
As butterflies flutter, in colorful flights.
Hovering hedgehogs crack all kinds of puns,
While frogs leap in rhythm, like they're having fun.

Reveries of Rustling Blades

Grass blades converse in a comical hum,
Tickled by footsteps, they giggle and strum.
The daisies are prancing, in frolicsome bliss,
While the sunbeams wiggle, a warm, golden kiss.

Ants march in lines, with a purpose anew,
Yet trip on their words, as they pile up their dew.
The breeze teases flies, a game of tag,
While the burbling brook shares tales with a brag.

Melodies in the Meadowlands

Robins compose songs, in a playful ballet,
While rabbits all bounce, in a swift cabaret.
The flowers all nod, in approval so grand,
As bees set the tempo, with buzzes unplanned.

With hiccups and chuckles, the sky joins the fun,
Clouds watch the antics and spin like a bun.
A family of foxes dance near a vine,
While the sun puts on shades, it's party time fine!

The Song of the Silent Stream

A stream so quiet, it holds a grin,
Fish gossip softly, the tales begin.
Bubbles rise up, with giggles inside,
Making the pebbles burst out to hide.

A frog in a tux, with a cane in hand,
He leaps like he's off to a big band stand.
The dragonflies buzz, play sweet little pranks,
Dancing in circles, giving the reeds thanks.

Lullabies of the Lazy Horizon

Sunsets yawn wide, a warm golden glow,
Clouds twist and turn, putting on a show.
The grass whispers secrets, in breezy delight,
While crickets tap dance into the night.

Squirrels chuckle, in their high-tree bars,
Trading old jokes about the moon and stars.
As shadows stretch long, they trip on their tail,
And tumble down laughter, they can't seem to fail.

The Soft Glow of Petal's Cradle

A flower wakes up, with a bright, silly blink,
It shakes off the dew, and gives a soft wink.
Bees buzz about, in their fuzzy parade,
Claiming sweet nectar, this day's grand charade.

Butterflies giggle, as they flutter and flit,
Calling all buds to join in a skit.
Petals fall down, like confetti on ground,
Each landing with charm, making joy abound.

Shadows Dancing on the Ground

In the day's warm glow, shadows start to play,
They bob and they weave, in a comical sway.
A dog tries to catch, what just can't be tamed,
Chasing his shadow, but it's not what he claimed.

Beneath the old tree, a whispering breeze,
Swings low the branches, like it's laughing with ease.
A squirrel takes notice, with a comedic flare,
He mimics the dance, but trips on thin air.

Calls from the Heart of the Green

In the grass, a bug does dance,
Singing loud, it takes a chance.
A cow nearby starts to moo,
Wishing it could sing, too!

The flowers giggle, petals bright,
Telling jokes from dawn till night.
A daisy winks, a tulip pouts,
As bees buzz by, and no one doubts.

A rabbit hops, a squirrel grins,
Playing tag where the fun begins.
With every hop and little leap,
They giggle softly, then fall asleep.

Vibrations of a Living Canvas

The daisies yell, "Oh, look at me!"
"Can't you see I'm wild and free?"
A sunflower twirls with sheer delight,
Chasing shadows, bold and bright.

Then comes the breeze with giggles low,
Tickling leaves with a gentle blow.
Grass blades whisper secrets with glee,
As critters join the symphony.

A bumblebee crafts a buzzing tune,
Under the playful gaze of the moon.
Each note rises, a riotous cheer,
Echoing loud for all to hear.

The Chorus of the Changing Leaves

In autumn's breeze, the leaves all chat,
"Did you hear the news? We're all going flat!"
They dance and chuckle, swirl in the air,
Making crowns for the critters to wear.

A squirrel sighs, "Oh, what a feat!
I must find nuts to make a sweet treat."
The acorns roll, they join the fun,
While birds gossip about the sun.

With every rustle, a brand new joke,
As pumpkins laugh beneath the oak.
The chorus swells, a merry sound,
As joy and laughter fly all around.

Elysian Sounds under the Sky

Under the wide, blue skies aglow,
A cricket plays a lively show.
A frog jumps in with a splashy tune,
And butterflies dance like a cartoon.

The clouds drift by, they giggle so,
Saying, "We're just here to steal the show!"
A rainbow grins from a lofty height,
Painting laughter in pure delight.

Even the sun hums a jaunty rhyme,
Warming the scene, as it keeps time.
With each chuckle, the world feels bright,
As nature's humor takes to flight.

Reflections of a Wistful Sky

In a sky so wide and blue,
Clouds gather, with not much to do.
One floats by, a lazy ghost,
While another's off to brunch, I boast.

Birds chirp tunes, a crooked note,
One's lost his way, can't find his coat.
Butterflies dance, but trip and fall,
Oh, nature's chaos—it's a free for all!

The Unseen Rhythm of Nature's Pulse.

Squirrels plot with nutty schemes,
Chasing shadows, chasing dreams.
A rabbit hops, with quite a flair,
Bumping into thin air, oh, despair!

The wind joins in, with a whoosh and swish,
As leaves rustle, they all wish.
A toad croaks loud, as if to say,
'Please stop, I'm trying to croak today!'

Whispers of Wildflowers

Daisies giggle in the sun,
While dandelions have too much fun.
They puff and blow, spreading cheer,
Little wishes fly, oh dear!

A bee bumps in, quite a clumsy flirt,
Gets tangled up in a yellow skirt.
Petals blush, as they softly sway,
Nature's dance, in a silly way!

Secrets Beneath the Grass

A worm wriggles, quite the sneak,
Digging deep, avoiding a peek.
He hears the gossip, oh so loud,
From ants marching, all so proud.

The blades of grass, they whisper low,
'Watch out for that funky toe!'
A rabbit snickers, hiding so sly,
Nature's secrets, oh my, oh my!

Nature's Gentle Lullaby

In the grass, a critter sneezes,
A chorus of bugs and breezy wheezes.
The flowers giggle, swaying with glee,
While clouds pass by, sipping herbal tea.

A squirrel on a branch starts to dance,
Chasing his tail, he takes a chance.
The sun winks, casting shadows wide,
As the brook chuckles, bubbling with pride.

Sighs of the Singing Earth

Birds gossip in treetops high,
While ants march by in a neat little line.
The daisies gossip, their petals aflutter,
As the wind tells jokes that make them mutter.

A rabbit rolls over, trying to hide,
From a sheep with a hat who just can't decide.
The rocks go rolling, having a blast,
While the sun laughs loud, this day's unsurpassed.

Petals in a Twilight Breeze

With a flap, a butterfly trips in the dusk,
Landing in tea, oh what a must!
The moths join in, a late night soiree,
While crickets strum loud, come join the play!

Dandelions whisper secrets so light,
As shadows dance, much to their delight.
The owls clap softly, they're wise and spry,
As the stars twinkle back, oh me, oh my!

The Soft Footfall of Cloud Shadows

Fluffy critters float overhead,
As shadows chase rabbits who might be misled.
The grass giggles underfoot, funny and shy,
While the daisies debate, "Should we wave or fly?"

A hedgehog rolls over, what a sight!
He dreams of tall tales, oh what a flight!
The sky bursts with laughter, it's light as a feather,
While the wind weaves stories, oh my, what a tether!

Footprints Beneath the Stars

I wandered out with shoes untied,
And tripped on grass, slipped, then cried.
The fireflies laughed, they danced about,
As I lost my way, I wiggled out.

The owls hooted, what a sight!
I tried to moonwalk, oh what a fright!
A raccoon clapped, he knew my plight,
I'd put on a show without a spotlight.

Beneath the moon, I tried to floss,
But tangled my feet—what a loss!
Stars glittered, chuckled from afar,
"Look at that fool, what a bizarre!"

Back to my path, I hopped and spun,
A comet zoomed, my night was fun!
The shadows snickered, they knew the art,
Of making me dance, a true work of heart!

Traces of Twilight's Kiss

In twilight's glow, I hear a snore,
A toad with dreams of being more.
He dreams of hops at the big parade,
But settles down; his plans do fade.

The crickets chirp a catchy tune,
They joke about the lazy moon.
I joined their band, not quite in key,
A song of smirks, they laughed at me!

The fireflies dressed in yellow glow,
Said, "Don't be shy, just let it flow!"
With bug-eyed friends, I did a jig,
And then tripped over a very big twig.

The sky turned dark, the stars took flight,
They winked at us, "What a delight!"
So let's just dance in this froggy mist,
And cherish what it means to exist!

Stories Carried by the Breeze

The wind whistled tales of bees,
Who wore striped shirts and sailed with ease.
They buzzed about, full of flair,
Teaching the flowers their funny air.

A dandelion, with seeds so bold,
Said, "Catch my dreams or so I'm told!"
But as he blew, his seeds took flight,
And landed on my nose—what a sight!

Laughter drifted on the warm air,
As butterflies flapped, spreading cheer everywhere.
They painted the sky with colors so bright,
While I sneezed loudly, oh what a fright!

Among the giggles of nature's choir,
I joined in the fun, fueled by desire.
So here's to the stories, both silly and sweet,
That float on the breeze, oh how they repeat!

A Symphony of the Salamander

In the cool wet grass, I found a band,
A funky crew of critters so grand.
With slippery bodies, they moved in time,
Making music that felt like a rhyme.

The salamanders played their scales,
A groovy beat that never fails.
Adding a twist with wiggly tails,
Even the shyest joined in with gales!

A flute from a frog, a drum from a snail,
Together they squeaked, a fidgety tale.
As I clapped along with a hop and a cheer,
A hedgehog peeked in, "What's up over here?"

So we jammed till dusk with giggles galore,
Creating a symphony, leaving us wanting more.
Nature's orchestra, the most absurd,
In the heart of the night, our joy spread like word.

Echoes in the Emerald

In the grass, a chipmunk pranced,
With acorns in hand, he took a chance.
Squirrel friends giggled, spinning around,
In a game of hide and seek, they proudly bound.

A butterfly sneezed, and they all just froze,
While a beetle in boots strutted, struck a pose.
The flowers were laughing, swaying in cheer,
As the sun set low, with a warm cavalier.

A little snail slid, and the ants sneered loud,
"Oh look, here comes the slowest in the crowd!"
But the snail just winked with a slimy, sly grin,
"You may be speedy, but I've got this win!"

Then a wise old crow, perched high on a tree,
Cawed jokes about worms, so funny and free.
His punchlines tickled the blooms in delight,
Echoes of laughter danced into the night.

Songs of the Sunlit Field

In sunshine's glow the daisies croon,
A cricket's tune makes the butterflies swoon.
They twirl in the air, putting on quite a show,
While bees buzz by with their sweet, sticky glow.

A wiggly worm sang a song without care,
And the grasshoppers chuckled, their tunes in the air.
A flamboyant rabbit, with a hat made of leaves,
Told stories of treasures behind the tall evens.

A dandelion puff, by a whisper was blown,
"Hey, look, I'm a drone, to the clouds I have grown!"
The petals all giggled, "Well, aren't you so grand!"
As they danced with the breeze in a zesty band.

Under the blanket of the bright, shining sky,
A wise old owl hooted, his feathers awry.
With a wink and a nod, he rapped with a beat,
"Join in, all you critters, let's groove to this heat!"

Breezes that Paint the Air

A gusty wind whispered through branches tall,
Tickling the flowers, inviting them all.
They giggled and swayed, in a colorful dance,
While a butterfly blushed in its bright polka pants.

A fox played a tune on his wrinkled old flute,
And the frogs joined in, hopping, not missing a beat.
With every ribbit, the sunflowers swayed,
As the clouds overhead formed a comedy parade.

A playful breeze painted smiles on the leaves,
While the ants on the ground plotted fun little thieves.
"Let's steal those seeds!" whispered one giddy mate,
"Or let's gather our snacks for a glorious bait!"

So the wind tickled cheeks, and they all laughed aloud,
Under green canopies, so lively and proud.
In this lively court, no leaf was forlorn,
Just breezes of joy with new tales to adorn!

Dances of Dandelions

Dandelions twirled in polka dot dresses,
With class and with flair, they gathered their guesses.
"What's next on the list?" asked a brave little sprout,
"A dance-off with clouds? Let's see what they're about!"

A bee took a chance, with his boogie so bright,
He buzzed and he whirled, such a marvelous sight.
The petals united and joined in the cheer,
"Let's toast to the sunshine, it's our time of year!"

A mischief of mice threw a cheese ball parade,
With squeaks of delight, they performed unafraid.
Each tumble and twist, a spectacle rare,
Spinning tales of delight in the soft, fragrant air.

So in fields where laughter danced with a breeze,
They celebrated life with relative ease.
For each funny moment, like dandelions' bliss,
Is a reason to giggle—there's joy in the mist!

Murmurs of the Wandering Wind

A gusty tickle goes by my ear,
Singing sweetly, loud and clear.
"Hey there, grass! How are you today?"
"Just swaying and laying! Hooray!"

Through crooked paths and wobbly trees,
The breeze spills laughter, floats with ease.
"Watch out, flower! Don't you sway too wide!"
"I can't help it, I'm a petal-pride!"

A dance of whispers along the way,
Each tiny critter breaks into play.
"Catch me if you can, you silly breeze!"
"No chance! I'm busy playing with bees!"

With every turn, a shout, a cheer,
The wind insists "I'm always near."
"I'm the jester of this earthy stage!"
"Join the fun, and turn the page!"

Whispers of the Whispering Woods

In wooded realms where giggles bloom,
Branches sway as they chase the gloom.
A squirrel shouts, "I'm king of this hill!"
"You wish! I'm the queen, so stand still!"

Mossy carpets cushion each prank,
Leaves rustle softly, giving a rank.
"Who knocked you over? Was it the owl?"
"Nope, just the wind! He's such a foul!"

Squirrels and bunnies, a comedic troupe,
Their antics turn the woods to a loop.
"Jump higher, critters, see who can glide!"
"Ooops, fell in the pond! Let's go for a ride!"

The trees keep chuckling, a leafy brigade,
As little feet scatter, none long delayed.
"Hey, don't forget to come back for snacks!"
"With winged companions, we'll avoid all hacks!"

A Symphony of Stillness

In the quiet glade, a frog takes a leap,
Carrying tunes of secrets to keep.
"Hey, what's that noise? A bird's tiny song!"
"Nope, it's my croak! I'm a singer, so strong!"

A snail slowly climbs, feeling quite grand,
"I'm the best at leisure—ain't life just planned?"
"With all that slow, you'll miss the best bite!"
"Oh please, I savor every tasty sight!"

Soft breezes hum as they float by the brook,
The fish give a wink, a sly little hook.
"Come join our splash! It's a fountain of fun!"
"Only if there's cake! Let's celebrate, run!"

The air is filled with each gentle cheer,
Laughter presents a bright atmosphere.
"Let's make a ruckus, the stillness can wait!"
"Agreed! Let's gather, it's time to create!"

Chimes of the Flowering Grove

In a grove where blossoms play peek-a-boo,
Petals giggle in every bright hue.
"Hey, Rosa! What's tickling your side?"
"Just this joker bee—he can't ever hide!"

Butterflies dance in a colorful whirl,
"Catch me if you can!" as they happily twirl.
"I can't chase you! My wings are too fat!"
"Then roll with me, let's do a bug spat!"

A ladybug laughs, perched high on a leaf,
"Tell me your secrets, oh sweet little thief!"
"Take a nap with me, let dreams light our way!"
"And then we'll party until the next day!"

The grove keeps chortling, with humor so bright,
From sun-kissed morn till the fall of night.
"Let's toast our joys with pollen-filled glee!"
"Tonight, I'll wear rhinestones, just wait and see!"

Threads of Twilight Tangles

Tangled shoelaces weave with glee,
Socks on heads, a sight to see.
Bouncing bees buzz out of tune,
Chasing giggles 'neath a moon.

Caterpillars break out in dance,
Twisting leaves in a wild prance.
Ants in line start doing the waltz,
Oh, the chaos! Who will pause?

Bunnies hop and boogie along,
Jumps to the beat of a silly song.
Grasshoppers join with a leap and a spin,
Each strum of laughter ignites a grin.

As twilight drapes in hues so bright,
All creatures prepare for a dance tonight.
With tangled threads, let revelry soar,
In this silly show, we want more!

Symphonies of the Silent Glade

In the glade where trees do sway,
Squirrels play their drum quite gay.
Mice put on a symphony show,
Hiding cheese in a major flow.

Frogs croak the beat, a ribbit tune,
While crickets chirp under the moon.
A snail conducts with a stick so fine,
As the groundhog croons, feeling divine.

Butterflies flutter, hats on their heads,
Making up jokes that dance like threads.
The flowers sway, swaying to sound,
In this silent glade, parody's found.

A raucous harmony fills the night air,
Nature's jesters without a care.
In laughter's embrace, the world feels light,
A festival of whimsy ignites the night.

Visions in Verdant Valleys

In valleys green, the sheep play chess,
Woolly kings dressed to impress.
While frogs judge with amused delight,
Picking the winners, all budding bright.

Dandelions sprout with a witty grin,
Crowning daisies, the queens of sin.
Laughter bubbles from every brook,
As turtles read the funniest book.

Streams gurgle jokes, oh so twinkly,
While bunnies munch on snacks so sprinkled.
Under the sun, they're a comedic crew,
Playing pranks in perfect view.

Every hill hums a playful tune,
Nature's folly, a joyous boon.
In verdant valleys, the mirth does swell,
With laughter and love, all is well.

Flutter of Wings Under Clouds

Wings flapping, birds began to tease,
Who can fly the highest with ease?
Doves in sunglasses lounge on a wire,
Laughing at clouds that never tire.

Parrots gossip, squawking with cheer,
Telling tales we'd love to hear.
With a flap and a pop, they make a show,
Dancing round rainbows, to and fro.

Breezy feathered friends jump with delight,
Swinging to the rhythm of day and night.
Clouds giggle, rolling just like a ball,
As laughter fills spaces, embracing us all.

So join this flutter, oh little bird,
For in joy's echo, let's be heard.
Under clouds that wander and roam,
Together, in laughter, we find our home.

Sunlit Secrets of the Wild

In sunlight's glow, the squirrels chat,
A pair of rabbits wear a hat.
They hide their snacks in shady nooks,
While singing songs in funny books.

Bumblebees buzz with goofy grins,
Claiming they're the best at spins.
A ladybug steals a flower's crown,
As ants parade her in the town.

The flowers giggle, petals sway,
While frogs dance waltz beneath the ray.
A cactus cracks a prickly joke,
As laughter floats in every poke.

Heartbeats Under the Stars

The owls hoot like they're up to tricks,
As fireflies flash their tiny flicks.
A raccoon dances on the table,
Declaring he's the biggest fable.

Crickets chirp a midnight tune,
While snails groan in their silver swoon.
A hedgehog plays the tambourine,
With all its spines, quite the machine!

Stars blink back at the forest night's show,
Where shadows sway and giggles grow.
A fox tells tales of curious things,
As laughter lifts on gentle wings.

Shimmers of Serenity in the Air

The butterflies wear polka-dot coats,
While dragonflies zoom like speedy boats.
A silly worm pops up to greet,
Wiggling to an unheard beat.

The sunflowers stretch, pretending to yawn,
As daisies dance at the break of dawn.
A grasshopper spins in a cheerful flip,
And the daisies join in for a floral trip.

Tails flick and giggles float by,
As petals whisper beneath the sky.
With every breeze, the laughter swells,
In nature's secrets, joy compels.

Nature's Gentle Gossip

The brook babbles with rumor and glee,
While the wind whispers back like a bee.
A feathered friend shares the day's tease,
Of a squirrel caught in a ticklish breeze.

The toads declare a hop-along race,
While lilies laugh in an elegant grace.
A playful breeze tugs at their stems,
As nature's children make silly gems.

With every rustle, stories unfold,
Of garden antics and secrets told.
In this world where laughter intertwines,
Gentle whispers bloom on sunny vines.

Harmony of Hummingbees

Buzzing round the flowers bright,
Hummingbees dance in pure delight.
They bumble, stumble, take a dive,
In pollen parties, they arrive!

Their tiny wings a comical sight,
Sip the nectar, oh what a bite!
But when they fight, it's quite a show,
Who knew they had such flair to blow?

With every buzz, they tell a tale,
Of sweet escapades without fail.
If only humans could take flight,
We'd share the fun, oh what a sight!

A harmony of giggles and glee,
In nature's circus, wild and free.
So raise a glass to buzzing cheer,
For hummingbees, we hold so dear!

Flickers of Light in Bloom

Fireflies twinkle like stars on ground,
Their dance is crazier than we've found.
With little winks, they play their games,
In summer nights, no two are the same.

One's taking a dip, the other's a flirt,
Lighting up flowers, skirts, and dirt.
They flicker, fumble, in a wild spree,
Best friends with the breeze, oh who can disagree?

They joke with crickets, trade silly puns,
While we mere mortals just wish for runs.
Their flickers weave tales of pure delight,
We watch in awe, feeling quite light!

In the garden of giggles, their laughter blooms,
Like tangled dreams amidst cartoonish toons.
So grab a jar, catch a bit of that light,
A whimsical glow to end the night!

The Serenade of Crickets

Crickets chirp their nighttime tune,
Underneath the bright, round moon.
They sing and dance in nightly bliss,
With a rhythm you can't miss.

Their leggy solos go on and on,
Yet for the audience, they just yawn.
"Do you hear that?" one may exclaim,
"Sounds like a weird cricket game!"

Not stars above, but critters below,
Join the chorus, even the crow!
Each note a giggle, each pause a tease,
Nature's band makes for quirky pleas.

Yet if they fail to keep fine tune,
They wobble and wobble, like a buffoon.
But that's the fun, it's wild and free,
In crickets' serenades, we smile with glee!

Tides of Tall Grasses

Tall grasses sway like dancers in line,
Bowing to breezes, oh how they shine!
They whisper secrets with every gust,
Foolish rabbits hear them and trust.

The swishing sound, a playful sweep,
More like a joke than promises deep.
They play hide and seek, it's their game,
But I'll never guess their tall tales' name!

Dancers in sunlight, they bob and weave,
Making fun of all who perceive.
The wind unwinds tales of playful prank,
Turning wise waltzs into a prank!

So sit awhile, and watch them sway,
Like sailors adrift in a sunny bay.
With laughter echoing under the trees,
The tides of tall grasses bring us ease!

Whispers of the Wildflower

In a patch of cheer, where daisies play,
A bee lost its way, turned flower bouquet.
With clumsy pirouettes in the sun's warm light,
He bumped a bright bloom, what a comical fright!

The poppies giggle as the wind passes through,
While dandelions snicker at the clouds' silly hue.
A ladybug trudges with a serious frown,
But slips on a petal, and tumbles right down!

Sunflowers sway in a dance they're contrived,
They gossip in whispers about bees they've connived.
They poke fun at the grasshoppers leaping so high,
While butterflies waltz, painting the blue sky!

Laughter erupts from the clover so green,
Tickled by tickles from bumblebee's sheen.
Amidst the blooms bright, the joy takes its stand,
With whispers of laughter that sprout from the land!

Secrets in the Tall Grass

In the tall grass where secrets conspire,
The ants hold a meeting, the stakes are much higher.
"Who stole the last crumb?" one cries with a shout,
While a wandering snail just shrugs and flouts!

A frog with a top hat conducts a grand show,
He croaks out a tune, and the crickets all flow.
In a symphonic clash, the bugs join his plea,
But the flies just roll their eyes, "Let us be free!"

The wind carries tales of a feathered row,
As sparrows argue over who's better at show.
With antics and banter they flitter and dive,
And tease the slow tortoise, who can't seem to thrive!

Underneath the tall blades, a cat stalks with glee,
But the mice all giggle, "Bet you can't catch me!"
With secrets that flourish in this whimsical space,
The grass is alive with a comical grace!

Symphony of the Sunlit Fields

In sunlit fields where butterflies dart,
The flowers hum tunes from the heart.
With petals a-swaying, they form a nice band,
A tune of the joyful, delightful and grand!

The grasshoppers leap in a tap dance delight,
While ants march along, keeping rhythm just right.
The sun beamed its smile, shining down on the song,
But a squirrel with sunglasses declared, "This is wrong!"

A cow joins in softly with a moo so bizarre,
She's dreaming of milkshakes and cheeseburgers afar.
The bumblebees buzz with their sweet serenade,
There's laughter and cheer, oh, this joyful parade!

As day turns to dusk, the crickets will croon,
While owls nod their heads to the whimsical tune.
And the fireflies flicker like stars all around,
With a symphony playing, pure joy can be found!

Echoes of the Gentle Breeze

With whispers so soft, the breeze gives a tickle,
Caressing the flowers and making them giggle.
The trees sway their arms, join in the fun,
As branches do the limbo beneath the bright sun!

A gust swirls around, pulling hats off with glee,
While squirrels laugh madly, "Now, that one's for me!"
They chase after leaves that whirl in the air,
Playing tag with the breeze, without a single care!

The dandelions puff, making wishes galore,
Each whispering seed let's out a tiny roar.
"Catch me!" they shout as they float with a flare,
Setting off on adventures, beyond everywhere!

As the day comes to close, with stars shining bright,
The echoes still linger, an enchanting delight.
For even the night has its own playful tease,
In the dance of the shadows, and laughs of the breeze!

Flickers of Light in the Quiet Glen

Butterflies dance, on a flower spree,
Chasing each other, just like kids at glee.
A bumblebee winks, takes a sip on the go,
While ants hold a meeting, just to say hi, though.

The shadows play tag, behind tall grass blades,
Sunbeams giggle, casting funny parades.
A squirrel slips up, in a comical fall,
While frogs sit in silence, judging it all.

A throne of toadstools, where the critters convene,
With raccoons in tuxes, so dapper, so keen.
The wind tells a joke, and the trees start to laugh,
As daisies grin wide, snapping their own photograph.

So here in the glen, where all antics unfold,
The critters in jest, share stories retold.
A chorus of chuckles, in the glow of the light,
Where laughter is free, and the fun feels just right.

Reverberations of the Chirping Crickets

Crickets compose, in harmonious strum,
A symphony's funny—who knew they were dumb?
One missed a beat, and they all start to sway,
As fireflies flicker, turning night into play.

A grasshopper leaps, decides to break dance,
Creating a circle, oh what a wild chance!
The owls roll their eyes, and prefer to just snooze,
While shadows of rabbits are having a ruse.

A cacophony bursts, with chirps of delight,
Each cricket a solo, in the dim moonlight.
The giggles of nature, echoing around,
As stars blink in rhythm, their twinkle confound.

With a wink and a nod, the night wraps it tight,
Crickets finish their concert, goodnight to the light.
They'll be back in the morn, to chirp once again,
Their rhythm infectious, a laugh 'round the glen.

Threads of Silk in the Serene Air

Spider webs shimmer, like jewels in the sun,
Spiders are seamstresses, having so much fun.
They twist and they spin, with a flair not discreet,
Creating fine art, where all the flies meet.

A ladybug hops, with her polka-dot show,
While a snail takes a selfie, moving way too slow.
The thrill of the chase, it's a game they all play,
And caterpillars giggle, as they munch through the day.

Breezes tickle noses, as they tiptoe and bop,
The flowers cheer in color, they're all just on top.
A worm gives a wink, as he wiggles on down,
Turning the soil with a smile, not a frown.

So amidst all this whimsy, with laughter and wiggle,
Nature holds its own, with a chuckle and giggle.
For in the tapestry, under skies so bright,
Life spins its silk, in pure comedic light.

The Gentle Sigh of Sun-Drenched Earth

Under the sun, the earth lets out a sigh,
A worm pokes his head, whispers, "Oh me, oh my!"
The daisies are gossiping, their petals all wide,
While squirrels play chess, with acorns as their guide.

Ants march in order, a parade with no end,
But tripping and tumbling, they're just 'round the bend.
The daisies all laugh, at the sight of their plight,
As the grasshoppers chuckle, oh what a delight!

A sunbeam peeks through, tickling cheeky plants,
While dragonflies dance, in their shimmery pants.
The earth speaks in whispers, of comical dreams,
Painting the land with bright, funny themes.

As shadows grow long, and the day starts to fade,
The insects continue, their nightly charade.
With a wink and a wave, the earth bids goodnight,
In the twilight of laughter, everything feels right.

Gossamer Dreams on the Horizon

In the tall grass, a squirrel prances,
Wearing a hat that sways and dances.
He chases after a butterfly,
That giggles and twirls as it tries to fly.

A frog dons shades, lounging by the creek,
With a wink and a smile, he's never meek.
He croaks a tune to the rhythm of time,
As dragonflies join in, mimicking rhyme.

Fragrance in the Folding Light

The flowers gossip in colors so bold,
Telling secrets that never grow old.
A bee in a tuxedo, quite the sight,
Buzzes around in his evening flight.

A bumble takes charge, leading the crew,
They dance in circles, what a hullabaloo!
With a flurry of petals, they put on a show,
While a wise old owl just hoots, "Let it flow!"

The Trill of the Thistle

A thistle sings songs with a raspy tone,
While nearby daisies giggle, never alone.
A rabbit with spectacles jots down the hues,
Of chortling critters in party shoes.

A cricket struts forth, now a dance king,
Challenging butterflies to join in and swing.
With a hop and a skip, they leap and they whirl,
While a breeze whispers softly, "Give it a twirl!"

Caresses of the Gentle Sky

The clouds play tag, light as can be,
While a chill breeze tickles a playful tree.
A pet rock claims it's a rare bird's nest,
Fooling the crows, who can't leave it rest.

Rain drops joke, "Look at us shine!
We're less of a storm and more of a line!"
And as the sun grins, giving them props,
They fall in a giggle, as moisture drops.

www.ingramcontent.com/pod-product-compliance
Lightning Source LLC
Chambersburg PA
CBHW071812160426
43209CB00003B/62